I0729888

in case of emergency press

We are proud to acknowledge the Traditional Owners of
country throughout Australia and to recognise their
continuing connection to land, waters, and culture.
We pay our respects to their Elders.

We support recognition, reconciliation, and reparation.

Just write about a bird

Ellie Cottrell

in case of emergency press
https://icoe.com.au
Travancore, Victoria
Australia

Published by in case of emergency press 2025

Copyright © Ellie Cottrell 2025
All rights reserved. Without limiting the rights under copyright
reserved above, no part of this publication may be reproduced,
stored in or introduced into a database and retrieval system or
transmitted in any form or any means (electronic, mechanical,
photocopying, recording or otherwise) without the prior written
permission of both the owner of copyright and the above publishers.

ISBN: 978-1-7637749-5-7

Cover Design: **Laura Parkinson**

Acknowledgements

Versions of the following poems have been published as follows:

'Freak Storm in Mandjoogoordap' in *StylusLit* 16
'The Grief in Living' in *Creatrix* 63
'Hubby' in *PULP Lit Mag: Paperback Romance*
'Noah from *The Notebook*' in *Poetry d'Amour* 2024
'There's Been Complaints' in *Stories with Pride* (Raine Square Short Story Dispenser & Writing WA 2024)
're: november 2014' in *PULP Lit Mag: Paperback Romance*
'Could Numbers Ever Know' in *Poetry d'Amour* 2023
'Apogee' in *Creatrix* 68

Many thanks to Writer Jackson for their thoughtful editing and feedback.

Special thanks to Kat Wray—Red Eclectic Photography

Dedication

For those who write, about anything.

Table of Contents

Just write about a bird

a bird

Ellie Cottrell

'Just write what you know'

My Twenties, in a Shot Glass

Sammy wore a silver ring. It was grease-slicked and shiny,
winking in the light as he shaped burger patties.
He was cool, Sammy, with his motorbike mo and
nonchalant lisp. I found it weird that he was married.

In between shifts I'd eat two packs of noodles,
a novelty with diminishing returns. But it was that
or half my rent on a gourmet burger made by Sammy
and his ring. Pumpkin and goats' cheese,
South African beef; pineapple and pancetta—
gross. Besides, I didn't eat meat.

One aimless Saturday I hitched a lift to the bottle-o
with Leah and Malcolm, Passion Pit blaring from the
speakers. 'Sleepyhead'. We *were* sleepyheads
but the night was a promise and Malcolm was cute.

Why do some memories linger for their lack
of action? Nothing happened, save
a midnight confession: Malcolm
felt the same way as me. I had a bad
boyfriend and a good conscience
but later I wished I'd kissed him.

For five years I got higher than the exosphere
drinking spiced rum and post-mix Coke, then
plying my molten lungs with menthols.
The night I met my husband, he smoked a whole pack.

I see my twenties as a set of yearbooks, dusty and dog-eared
on a crooked shelf. The cast of characters is balding now,
or ripe with babies, or somewhere unreachable. Still,
I don't need to read the books to remember:

Sammy's ring, winking in the light.
Malcolm's smile—so kind—before he lost his mind.

Belonging, as a need

Those shirtless boys hollering in trees, eighteen and feinting, tough-but-not-really, waiting for something to happen. Precocious love schooled me, wrongly, that meaning comes in a boy shape. And so they take their hold.

Everything's golden, at this hour. The waning sun. The hollering boys. Two puddles of beer on the stage. A quiet longing lives under my skin.

In another life—one that looks like mine, but smaller—I climb the trees they've claimed. I swing my shirt in the air and scream for the band. I bask in their acceptance.

In another life—one that looks like mine, but bolder—I climb the trees they've claimed. I smile into the leaves. I lean back on a lusty branch, and watch the band begin.

Freak Storm in Mandjoogoordap

The night we stayed a storm
rolled in, rain heavy on the roof

I teased you for your furrowed brow
you teased my bold excitement

Crackling like the atmosphere
we chanced the outdoor bathtub—
'If lightning hits we're fucked'

Bubbles, thunder, give me a kiss

We took each other to the
outhouse, umbrella held aloft
I went first, then you (of course)

Laughing, shush, cover your eyes

When the rain got too much
we locked ourselves away—
'Is this your favourite date?'

Pillows, blankets, cuddle me please

First-light rays on shiny leaves
storm like a fever dream

You'd swear it never happened,
but for the smell of the earth

I am not Lily Allen

Parisian men
surrounding me
and chanting
'Lily Allen'

'Li-ly! Li-ly!'
They dance with
hands conjoined
at the Moulin Rouge

'Je suis… not Lily'
I counter lamely, in
my bright red dress
with my Lily Allen hair

For a moment
at the Moulin Rouge
I feel proper famous—
I am not a British pop star,

but you try telling them

At Lake Pukaki

We pulled up
at Lake Pukaki
we had it to ourselves

The lake was gorgeous,
otherworldly
her hue was pure azure

(Later we learned
it was the glacial flour—
joked we'd sneak some home)

Two hours later
a lone man drove in
he didn't meet our eyes

"He's a serial killer"
you whispered
I hated you for that

Through the long silent night
we stayed side by side
together, yet apart

When he left
just after sunrise
we were glad to see him go

Skin Check

Starburst on my neck.
'Irregular,'
the doctor says.

It whispers two clues
from his CHAOS poster
(an acronym, I assume,
although I can only connect
the A to 'asymmetrical').

'Hmmm.'
'Hmmmmmmm.'
'Yes, this needs a closer look.'

My body: a constellation.

At six o'clock on Wednesday
a nurse will blot out the star
before a scientist searches the crater.
And it does feel chaotic,
this scheduling of an incision.

My body: a star map

or maybe a poster,
the clues leading to chaos.

'Just write what you feel'

Polaroid (Nandi and Pa)

Together the couple stand squinting,
his hair a ruffled pompadour;
her cardigan, mint green,
with just one button done.

You know, I never
saw her in that shade.

It's a photo that, today
might be thrown away.
Taken in the seconds before
the winning smile, the 'sparkle'—
clouds like inkblot marshmallows
dot the sky behind them.

Still, my grandpa cuts
a rakish figure—even with
that pilled blue jumper.

And she could have
been a model, Nandi—
the name we always called her.

Together, my grandparents
stand squinting—so glam
in their fifties slacks.
Did Elvis inspire Pa's hair?

You know, I never
thought to ask.

The Grief in Living

There's a grief deep within me
I don't know where it's from

I feel it walking past
cafés I only
went to once
I feel it walking by
the house I leased
for months and months

It bubbles in
my throat, my chest
It's rooted at the heart
I guess it has
to do with time,
so swiftly in the past

The Year of Goin' Through It

The year of goin' through it
was birthed on a potholed
highway, a stretch of road
with no horizon.
Today's word is *scared*.

Dread so exquisite, so
sudden—immaculate
conception in the depths
of my chest.

Then the panic, ragged
at the edges and barely
contained—I worried the cause,
one fist clench away.

In the year of goin' through it
my mind sent a missile
with a message for my heart:
'There's no point
in beating much longer.'
Today's word is *numb*.

For a while the missile won
but then I searched the wreckage.
Today's word is *safe*.
Today's word is *calm*.
Today's word is *trust*.

It was words that got me through,
the year of goin' through it.

Safe

I am safe in my sun-drenched
room, my cotton-clad
skin, my love's broad
arms. I am safe

on sandy paths, a midday
train, looking
at a neon
sign. I am safe

with trees that flower
purple, smiles
that summon laughter,
something in my cup.

Hubby

I don't have the patience
for yearning or quiet desire—
I'm hot from first look till I split
my thrice-bitten lip

Your aunty bought us pillows
they say hubby, wifey
I'll take the hubby pillow
and you can be the wifey

I'll wear the hubby things
like your cologne:
a kiss on my wrist,
a pulse in my pocket

You'll wear the wifey things
like my softness:
soft hands on your chest,
soft lick of your neck

Together we'll be
hubby and wifey
no patience for yearning—
just desired, and desiring

'~~Just write about a bird~~'
'~~Just write what you know~~'
'~~Just write what you feel~~'
'Just write'

Noah from *The Notebook*

My introduction to love
was not through a kiss,
but an upskirt.
'I can see your undies,'
you said to me, staring.

New Year's Eve, 2004—
that was the night we first met.
Your voice was high-pitched
and I pitied you, but then
you looked up my skirt.

Me on the swings, flying.
You on the ground, staring.

Your voice was deeper
the next time we met—
Me standing over you,
hands on my hips.
You on the steps,
eyes on my lips.

'Sexy,' you muttered;
I remember that well.

I wasn't used to stubble,
but you kissed me so
heated I liked it.
Those days of sweetly
corrupted innocence
plagued me, a long time.

You were Noah from *The Notebook,*
The One That Got Away.
You were young love,
true love, something
like that—until one day

you weren't. You were just the weird kid
who looked up my skirt.

Two Tiny Flowers

1.

Buying veggies
at Coventry Market
we were brand new
he hadn't lied to me yet

Making out in the line
to buy a wilted leek
our hands clutched tight
and everything, magic.

2.

A rambling late-night call
exchanging sweet lie-things
'We're going to be together
a long time, aren't we?'

It was a shorter call
that ended it—I was
at work, too (the prick)
still, if I'm honest about it

I don't think about him much
but I guess when I do
there were two tiny flowers
that sprang from the shit

There's Been Complaints

'I'm sorry,' the barista said, discomfort etched on his face. 'There's been complaints. Can you please... stop that?'

Stop kissing, he meant. We were in a thrumming late-night coffee shop—the kind that doesn't exist anymore. Bright lights, posters on the walls. Pool table against my back as we cooed and caressed like doves.

At eighteen, I'd kissed boys in rain-slicked beer gardens; in cinemas and parks.

There were never any complaints before her.

While I knew he was only the messenger, I kept the message he delivered like kindling. It took me a decade—more—to burn it.

Anatomy Lesson

My heart hoards dust from old stars
and mildew from tears that never quite dried;
my mind has cobwebs in corners
and crud in the nooks—things to be dislodged.

My lungs have been blackened by a thousand
special cigarettes, made pink again
through a thousand sprinted staircases.

My hands have veins that snake back to
simpler times, but the bruise on my thumbnail
is new. My legs are strong as an ox
and dimpled on top, because
both these things can be true.

Little crows rest by my eyes,
twitching their feet with each smile;
fault lines trace parts of my face
but I'm whole, in spite of it all.

re: november 2014

texting *you mean the world to me*
with the globe emoji   the one
that shows australia

cos you were in kansas   of all places
and i was in perth   of all places
and i needed to feel like
we were on the same earth

squirming   to jump
through the screen   hurting
to touch your face
in 3d   hurting
like the pixels
were bullying me

god   that yearning
i wanted to drown
in your eyes   suffocate
in your chest hair   i wanted
to superglue my hands to your dick
and forget   every word
except *you*

Could Numbers?

Three thousand
one hundred
and two.

(It's how many days
I've spent
loving you.)

I can't quite grasp
a number that size:
numbers are cold, like

all the nights
I slip shivering into
bone-numbing sheets

and anchor myself
to you, your warmth,
my port in the storm.

Numbers are stark
but we are soft—
softly holding, softly gazing,

softly knowing.
Could numbers ever hold
the sum of their parts?

The sum of three thousand
one hundred and two
kisses, laughs, you-make-me-so-happys,

sorrows, regrets, I-wish-I-hadn't-said-thats
a blustery beach sunset at the perfect day's end;
crying in fear at the loneliest hour

Numbers couldn't hear
the choke in your throat
when you made me your wife

Numbers couldn't see
the smile in my eyes
when I said
'I'm ready.'

Honeymoon Robe

You drifted by in the hallway
wearing your honeymoon robe
Twice you did this
like a ghost, no answer
to my cries

I woke unsettled,
almost bereft
wondering what it meant:
In four sleeps' time
our marriage will turn two.

Years ago my
mother told me
'Long-term love,
it ebbs and flows'
Our tide's been coming in

Maybe the dream
was a whispered reminder,
a lucky charm on my path:
my *love*. What a present
your presence is

Raf's Dream

'I dreamed you were pregnant,' Raf says, meaning in his eyes.
I'm panting from the run. I'm panting at the thought. He mixes
my iced coffee in that special way of his: two teaspoons
dancing together. A whorl of ice and milk, then a bloom of
coffee, darkening. He doesn't even watch the spoons, so
practised is the dance. But I can't look away. Raf and his
spoons always make the perfect shade.

'Do your dreams ever come true?' I ask, uncertain of his
answer. Uncertain what I'd like the answer to be. I've been
dreaming of pregnancy since before my first blood—and yeah,
I guess I grieve when I wake up.

But then, I like my coffee *strong*. I like to run so hard I pant.
I like my belly flat.

'Well, every now and then,' Raf replies, in his sweet Brazilian
lilt. In today's novelty t-shirt. With his gently thinning
mohawk. His gently laughing smile. Sometimes Raf talks about
military school and how it fucked him up, which makes me
trust him more. I'd put stock in a dream he had. I'd bet money
on a dream he had.

I collect my coffee, other hand almost reaching for my belly.
Instinctively. Silly. All that's there is air and guts. Perhaps all
there'll ever be.

'You'd be the first to know.'

Apogee

Inspired by 'The Shuttle' by Andrew Rovenko

She stares out the window on her way to the moon.
Her helmet's papier mâché, but only I know that—
her father told me as we boarded the bus.

As she sits stiff-backed on the peeling
vinyl seat, I wonder at her tranquillity.
Can she really be so calm?

She's only eight years old.

Near the cosmodrome, the bus gathers speed.
The driver's excited, I guess. Outside, Earth rushes by
like it's upset she's leaving. 'It's not forever,'

I want to say, but I can't promise Earth that.
When we get off, there are news crews and shouts,
a storm of questions for the little astronaut.

(Will there be storms on the moon? I worry for her helmet.)

At the grandstand, I sit next to her father. His face
glistens with tears and something like pride.
'She wore her favourite shoes,' he sobs.

Her sneakers do look cool with her spacesuit
but I would have thought she'd need boots.
When she enters the rocket, he runs.

At blast-off, my binoculars fog with tears.
I knew nothing of space, at eight—
but the world wasn't dying then.

(Later, I learn there aren't storms
on the moon. It doesn't have weather at all.)

See You Out There

My greys are coming in
tinsel, Kelly calls them
I'm fascinated by
the caves under your eyes
(wanna go spelunking?)

We're cherub-faced forever
in my mind—
the mirror lies
long shadows
flank our memories

Back in the double oh's
I shared the starriest sky
I'd seen
with a boy I
did not want—
poor thing.

He knew his lack, I'm sure.

Even now when Venus
flaunts her showy shiny
pelt, I remember that night
and by extension, you
You, the strangest stranger

Still, I'll see you out there
in whatever way that means—
in dusty pics, unbidden dreams,
a thought out of the blue,
the thread of time stretched taut
and tight

(I'll be seeing you)

Everything's a Poem

Pavements stickered
with chewing gum
a world-weary cashier
on the red-eye shift

Snow-lidded mountains
pine needles scattered
on rain-drenched earth
your face in repose
as you start up the car

Fog rolling in
as the dawn road unfurls
disappearing
just as suddenly,
like an inhaled breath

Everything

About the Author

Ellie Cottrell is a writer and poet working on Whadjuk Noongar Country. Her writing has appeared in *Meniscus Literary Journal*, *PULP Lit Mag*, *StylusLit*, *Poetry d'Amour* and elsewhere. **Just write about a bird** is the follow-up to her debut poetry collection, **Speakeasy**, also published by *in case of emergency press*.

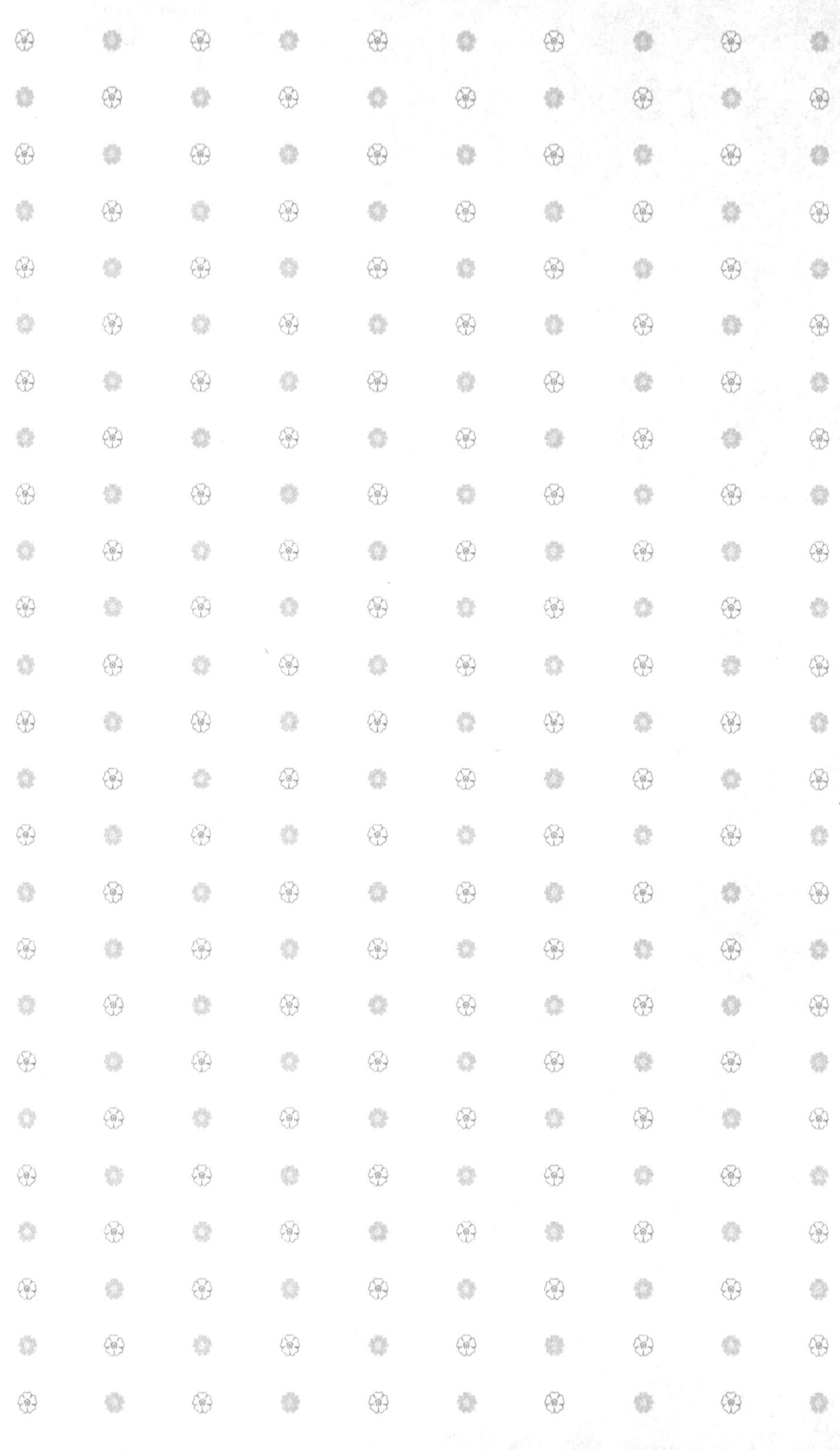

www.ingramcontent.com/pod-product-compliance
Lightning Source LLC
Chambersburg PA
CBHW051828180726
48283CB00004BA/1353